Benjamin Goodkind

Ben's travels, poems and essay

Benjamin Goodkind

Ben's travels, poems and essay

ISBN/EAN: 9783337209964

Printed in Europe, USA, Canada, Australia, Japan

Cover: Foto ©Andreas Hilbeck / pixelio.de

More available books at **www.hansebooks.com**

⇒BEN'S⇐

TRAVELS,

POEMS,

AND

By Benjamin Goodkind

ESSAY.

CHICAGO:
CO-OPERATIVE PRINTING ASSOCIATION.
1880.

PREFACE.

TO THE READER.

DEAR READER: After having gone through trials innumerable, and after having overcome obstacles that to me seemed insurmountable, I am at last enabled to place my little volume before you.

Every person whom I know, and many I do not know have advised me to discard literature, for two good and sufficient reasons. Firstly, because I do not know enough, and secondly, because I would never earn enough at it to buy a dinner. Despite their able arguments I clung to my own ideas however, and leaving every one whom I knew, betook myself to solitude and there studied incessantly. I endured the most pinching penury and want. This course of action of mine to my friends seemed so foolish and crack-brained that they deemed me demented. and frequently hinted at lunatic asylums, &c. I avoided them all though and persevered in my resolution to become an author. I knew I had the taste and inclination for literature, and these I deemed sufficient reasons to justify me in following out my aims. I felt convinced that I would never be a successful merchant (my friends' opinion to the contrary notwithstanding) because I never had a taste for business. I have struggled hard against my dislike for it, but in vain.

At first I concluded to devote myself to poetry entirely and make my debut as an author of rhymes, but I am convinced that the undertaking would be too difficult. It is not an easy matter to win a fair degree of success at prose writing, but at rhyming the chances at the outset are ten to one against success. When young I took a delight in rhyming and that feeling has clung to me ever since. I love to express myself in short, pithy sentences, and find that rhyme is admirably adapted to that purpose. I think that rhyming is an easy matter when you determine beforehand what you wish to say. At least I find it so. The first consideration is to have an idea, the second consideration to express it. The majority of my poems are melancholy. I am sorry to say that melancholy has become a confirmed trait of my character. Perhaps other scenes and a little sunshine will change that mood.

I am not at all sanguine as to my success at the start. I do not expect to be as lucky as Byron, who woke up one morning and found himself famous. No; I am content to win my way to success, if I win it at all, slowly and gradually.

Much that I have written I have destroyed, not deeming it worthy of notice. Several compositions now contained in my book, one of which is the "Ode to Melancholy," I also contemplated destroying, yet, had I done so, my book would have been more meager than it is, and it is meager enough now in all truth.

There is no great merit in my sketch entitled "My travels in Germany." The only merit I claim for it is truth.   Yours truly.

                                                    BEN.

CONTENTS.

POEMS.

BEN'S POEMS.

MY AFFINITY.

A DREAM.

EXPLANATION: Soon as the imagination begins to
ripen we all form to ourselves some beau ideal of the
fair spirit which we desire as our earthly minister,
and somewhat capriciously proportion our admiration
to living shapes according as the beau ideal of our
fancy is more or less approached. Beauty of a stamp
that is not familiar to our dreams may win our
homage, but it does not kindle an emotion that almost
seems to belong to memory itself. In this poem of
mine I have endeavored to portray the beau ideal of
my fancy, yet such a vague, shadowy phantom of the
brain will not bear a too close transcription.

THE DREAM.

'Twas on a gloomy winter morn,
Just when day began to dawn,
That a maiden stood and gazed intent
Upon the cheerless firmament.
She stood upon a lofty ledge
That uprose from the water's edge
Many hundred feet below—
Down there the northern sea did flow,
Far, far away as one could see
All was vague immensity.
In the atmosphere dull gray
Great clouds scurried light away.
Those wayward children of the air
Swept impetuous here and there.

11

From north and south and east and west
They ever eager onward pressed.
In the distance down below
Ceaselessly the sea did flow,
Ceaselessly did it flow on
To where it met the horizon.
There the fast approaching day
Was creeping up the heaven gray.
Soon a fitful light was seen
(With a scarce developed sheen)
'Pon a huge cloud's ragged edge—
'Twas Aurora's morning pledge.
Quick rose the wind loud to proclaim
That at last the morn had came.
Blythe and merry then it whistled,
And shrilly piped and deeply sizzled.
Then it 'gan to weep and wail,
And worked itself into a gale.
And now the cold green sea below,
Its mettle also fain would show.
It angrily began to roar,
And lashed the lonely, rocky shore.
Into the caverns waveworn, wild,
It surged with bold and mighty tide.
The hollow caverns loud did groan
And boom as if with thunder tone.
The winds more loudly then would hiss
And yell as if with greater bliss.
The billows leapt the higher with rage
And deadliest warfare seemed to wage.
But now the lingering sun arose
And watched amused the silly foes.
Her face crimsoned o'er with glee
And beamed with much benignity.
High and higher she came dancing
Rendering nature bright—entrancing.
Her beams were scattered left and right
And flooded ev'rything with light.
She awoke the gray sea mew
Which screamed as o'er the wave it flew.
The gannet, curlew, pyot—all
Wakened to her morning call.

The bold and rugged promontory
She clothed in a robe of glory.
She drove the gloom of night away,
And ushered in the full bright day.

While thus the maiden stood intent,
Gazing 'pon the firmament,
A wailing sound came from below—
A sound of utter human woe.
It came not from the yelling wind,
That still railed on with passion blind,
And beat against the promontory,
Which stood silent in its glory;
It came not from the booming cave,
Eternal lapped by ocean wave,
In whose recesses, hidden deep,
Creatures strange their vigil keep;
Nor came it from the rocky shore,
Upon whose strand forevermore
The surging water spends its force
And sudden checks its headlong course.
It was an infant's moving wail,
Borne upward by the morning gale.
The child was to the waves a prey,
Which bore it to the sea away.
Its tiny arms were outstretched,
As if in an appeal wretched.
Its frame hither, thither tossed,
'Neath a mighty wave seemed lost.
The maiden from the ledge on high
Downward cast her pitying eye.

Whish!! something darted thro' the air,
Crash!! something struck the water there.
Something through the waves did glide
Deep into the sea caves wide.
The waters o'er it steamed and boiled
Bubbles formed and eddies whirled.
The tumult tho' soon being o'er
The waves rolled onward as before.
At length the deep its prey upheaving

Two white arms quick 'gan cleaving
The mighty waters strong aside—
The girl had braved the ocean's tide.
From the dizzy, dangerous height,
(To look up even dazed the sight)
The girl had boldly downward leapt,
For pity in her heart had crept.
She gazed about then swam away
To where the helpless infant lay.
She nerved her arms so frail yet fair,
And gathered strength from sheer despair.
When down three times the child had went
She grasped it; but its life was spent.
At all events though she would save
Its body from a watery grave.
Once more she braced those arms so fair
And gained the shore by fortune rare.
The infant lay beside her dead—
All signs of life from it had fled.
No words her misery could tell—
No woe like her's is known in hell.
She hugged the child against her breast
And closer strained and closer prest.
She kissed its lips, its hands, its eyes,
The while half choked with sobs and sighs.
She laughed, she wept, she raved in turn,
And in her eyes hot tears did burn.
But what availed her sorrow sore?—
The child breathed not one breath the more.
She regarded sad the waters wide,
And low and piteously then cried.
The mighty but yet cruel ocean
Heeded not her deep emotion.
No pity did its voice express—
What cared it for her distress?
The wind still yelled unceasingly,
And seemed to mock her misery.
The sea birds swept all heedless by.
And had for her no pitying eye.
E'en the air, most piercing cold,
Not one pang from her would withhold.
Pity, pity there was none

From anything beneath the sun.

The maiden's form was round and lithe,
And yielding as a willow wythe.
Each limb appeared as if love set—
A glimpse of it would love beget.
Her thigh was full and fairly broad,
And with power seemed well stored.
Her ankle was as thin as paper,
But broadened as it up did taper.
Her tiny feet were good to view,
And had a salmon fish's hue.
Her mouth was like a rosebed red,
In which only sweets are bred.
Her breath was fragrant as a flower
When moistened by a summer shower.
Her eyes were of a clear light blue—
Love suffused them through and through;
In their depths flowed poetry
In unmeasured quantity.
When gazing 'pon their lovely sheen
They conjured up a summer dream
Where all is hope and joy and light
And unspeakable delight.
Their hue was sweet as wife's first child
Which 'pon her knee sits and doth smile,
And foolish crow and goo and gaa
And try to say " papa! mama!"
They were just as sweet as marriage night,
That time of most intense delight,
When waves of bliss rise higher and higher,
Then in a slippery sea expire.
Her voice was soft as music strains,
Whose thrilling, well-attuned refrains
Soothe the moonlit autumn night,
And call up mem'ries golden, bright.
'Twas clearer far than songs Tyrolean,
And softer far than harps Æolian.
But now her voice no joy did know—
Her heart, alas! had burst with woe.
She wailed. 'Twas like the gale

That sobbing soughs o'er northern seas.
She moaned. I heard the winds arise
From the mighty ocean's tide.
They gathered from the sea caves pride,
And, mingling in a hollow heap,
They swept the air and pined;
And did fret, lament, aud weep.
Then gathering for a tornado sweep,
They moaned low and lower,
Then sunk. Suddenly howled, howled, howled,
And boomed, and boomed, and boomed,
And crashed, CRASHED—collapsed.

MARTHA.

A SCOTTISH LOVE SKETCH.

I knew a Scottish Highland maiden
Whose waving auburn hair was laden
With smell of fragrant fresh-mown hay,
Her eyes! dancing little elfs were they.
Her mouth was just a ripe red rose,
But far more luscious, goodness knows.
Upon her lips there sat love's dew
Begging the fond swain to woo.
No shape like hers was ever found,
It was so lithe, and firm and round.
Her carriage was so queenly—great,
To see it would your sight elate.
Scarce sixteen years the lassie knew
And though innocent yet saucy too.
She had, Oh! *such* a spirit
That e'en the wild winds might well fear it.
That spirit lofty and so bold,
Dared men to bend it or to mold.
Unto herself did Martha vow
Never to man's will to bow.
She stubbornly resolved to rove,
(Like deer on the Highland heights above)
In undisturbed felicity:

Untrameled, wild, alone and free.
This lassie innocent, yet wild,
By worldly arts was undefiled.
She knew not fear, nor grief, regret,
And had no hopes to make her fret.
She cared not for the laddies braw—
" Would give no whustle for them a'."
Her confidence she would not share,
Not she indeed. " No ne'r! no ne'r!"
There came a lad, in years not old,
With pensive air, of pleasing mould—
A sentimental sort of creature,
With romance writ on ev'ry feature.
Insensibly a strong love chain
Ere long bound this confiding twain.
The lassie much did storm and frown,
But, sad to tell, love would not down.
Her mood, ever blithe and jolly,
Now gave way to melancholy.
Alas! alas! her spirit wild
Now was tame as any child.
She only cared for solitude
To there beguile her lonely mood.
From her heart, oppressed drear,
Ever rose the passive tear.
Continually she did pray
For death to carry her away.
Her face grew pinched, thin, and pale,
And her health began to fail.
She grew listless and supine,
And her eyes were red with cryin'.
Her pride! where to did it flee so fast?
She stood perplexed, amazed, aghast.
Her mind was sorely racked and riven,
And to consternation given.
Endless she did sigh and brood,
Till suddenly she changed her mood
And said: " This passion I will kill!
I'll kill it, an' I will, I will!"
She secured each truant tear,
And banished every sneaking fear.
She murdered ev'ry struggling sob,

And bade her heart less wildly throb.
She fierce suppressed those wicked sighs,
And dried her dancing elfin eyes.
Each and every harmless sniffle
Ruthlessly she tried to stifle.
Though her heart felt much oppressed
And fluttered wild within her breast,
Yet Cupid stern was reprimanded.
And to fly away commanded.
The Highland lassie wished to rove
Unfettered by the god of love.

TO THE WEEPING WILLOW.

1.

Willow, willow, wherefore weepest
  Thou ever o'er the graves of men?
Oh, how steadfastly thou keepest
  Thy lonely vigil over them.

2.

The long years come and then they go,
  And still thou stand'st untired by;
Thou see'st nought but human woe,
  And pain and grief and misery.

3.

Is it therefore that thou droopest,
  And weepest on forever more;
Is it therefore that thou stoopest,
  So sadly o'er the moldering corse?

4.

Oh, willow, willow, cease your sighing
  For souls that from this earth have fled;
There is a pleasure sweet in dying—
  For happy only are the dead.

5.

On this earth there is too much sorrow
  For sensitive and loving hearts;
They hope to-day, despair to-morrow,
  And yet are made of finest parts.

6.

Yes, willow, willow, cease your sighing
  For the unconscious happy dead;
Life's poetry begins when dying,
  When all earthly feeling 's fled.

THE INFLUENCE OF GENIUS UPON FAME.

1.

In Truth is Fame the fickle goddess,
  For she seldom smiles at will;
Altho' to rule her very hard is—
  Win her, she'll not treat you ill.

2.

Our goddess when in love is tender,
  And knows well how to allure;
To Genius doubtless she'll surrender,
  If the FLAME in him is pure.

3.

But 'tis not the poetic dreamer
  Who shall win her prized embrace;
Nor shall the bard of odd demeanor
  In her heart obtain a place.

4.

All at first will she receive,
  (Oh but she's a sly coquette!)
Yet many of them she'll deceive,
  Then their love will hate beget.

5.

Hosts of lovesick mortals woo her
　In many curious ways;
They all come rushing eager to her,
　With their stories, poems, plays.

6.

To be in first they lively scramble,
　And rude shove each other by;
Their glaring eyeballs savage ramble
　O'er the field of rivalry.

7.

The goddess to one bard says: "Friend,
　I own I love your chiming lays;
But alas! you've much to mend
　Ere you'll earn my honest praise."

8.

Then bowing, scraping, comes another,
　To whom she makes this love avow'l:
"Your verse is sad enough, my brother,
　To make e'en a dead dog howl."

9.

A third advances, sweetly smiling—
　Full of confidence is he;
She says to him: "Your verse beguiling
　Smells too much of pedantry."

10.

A fourth comes eager to the scratch—
　A novelist from France;
"Miss Fame," says he, "let's make a match;
　With me life's a romance."

11.

The goddess says: "Notoriety, here,
　(My sister) seeks a lover;
Take her, oh my novelist dear—
　Your affinity you'll discover."

12.

Thus the army comes, advancing,
  To the goddess, one by one;
At each one's merits quickly glancing,
  To her gude man she doth come.

13.

She finds a bard whose beaming eye
  Is full of Genius fire;
She finds 'tis her affiinty—
  The god of her desire.

14.

She calls him to her lofty throne,
  And throws o'er him the laurel;
The rest they make a rush for home.—
  Good folks, pray heed the moral!

AN APOSTROPHE TO THE MUSE.

1.

My own beloved steadfast Muse,
  Oh pray forsake me not.
I feel unhappy; don't refuse
  To cheer my miserable lot.

2.

Why feels my heart so very sad?
  What, oh what can cheer me?
In truth I am a luckless lad,
  For joy comes not oft near me.

3.

My love for you folks deem most strange—
  All tell me to forsake you;
But my devotion cannot change—
  My Muse, I'll never shake you.

4.

I might have been a richer lad
  Had I a taste for barter;
Unhappily I never had
  A bias in that quarter.

5.

And thus I'm doomed to live alone—
  By no one e'en respected;
Friends, companions I have none—
  By kinfolks e'en neglected.

6.

Yet, oh yet I won't despair,
  But stubborn struggle on;
I'll never halt, I firm declare,
  Till my destined task is done.

7.

Some friends grieve while others sneer,
  And some deem me demented.
For those who grieve I have a tear—
  Their grief, I much lament it.

8.

But yet my fate I cannot change,
  My taste I cannot alter;
I love my task, however strange,
  And must not, cannot falter.

9.

No! come joy or woe, sun or rain,
  My conscience I'll obey;
Come hunger, misery, or pain,
  Its voice I cannot drive away.

10.

This is a dreary, heartless world—
  Hope now, despair to-morrow;
When for wisdom we have toiled
  It doth bring us only sorrow.

11.

I'm quite sick of the hollow cant,
  Called " worldly education;"
To me it seems a comfort scant—
  A sad conglomeration.

12.

Some men will swear by all things dear
  They love you like a brother;
To say so they've an object clear—
  Some selfish aim or other.

13.

Fair women call upon the fates
  To witness how they love you;
Soon you'd flee to Barbary States,
  So that they can't reprove you.

14.

If you're rich then folks will flatter
  And shamelessly deceive you;
The more money that you scatter
  The kinder they'll receive you.

15.

But when the shekels all are spent
  Your best friends will desert you;
It is too late now to repent—
  Adversity hath virtue.

16.

Oft fame endeavors to allure
 Fools to its treach'rous light.
Did fame ever yet secure
  A man from hate or spite?

17.

Some patient mortals learn to rhyme,
  And thus seek gold or glory;
It is in truth a waste of time—
  Youth, wait until you're hoary.

18.

The best of rhymes are only words
  That flow with music measure;
Their harmony to some affords
  Perhaps an hour's pleasure.

19.

Put good sense into tuneful verse,
  Or put it into story;
THEN you've a chance—to put it terse—
  To capture sneers or glory,

20.

But now, my wearied, tortured Muse,
  I'll cease this rambling strain;
Its incoherence, pray, excuse—
  I'll not offend again.

LOUISE.

I knew a girl in by-gone time,
Who came from Albion's foggy clime.
To know her was to know but joy,
She was so fairy-like and coy.
Her voice was clearer than a flute,
And tender as a soft-stringed lute.
When she laughed the merry strain,
Made the welkin ring again.
The laughter's strain at first was soft,
Then it rippled up aloft,
And trill, and trill and trilled away,
Sweet as music e'er could play.
Her eyes were of that clear, deep blue

Which one in arctic skies can view,
Her hands were shapely small and white—
Her form, love rounded, graceful, slight,
Her ankle, tapering and trim,
Would lure a pious man to sin.
In short, she was a lovely flower,
Whose proper place was in the bower.
Though we may never meet again,
Louise, thy image I'll retain.

ALL IS DEAD!

1.

The wind is mournfully crying—
The trees are bending and sighing—
The dreary winter is dying—
    All is dead! dead! dead!

2.

What are the winter winds saying?
And why so turbulent playing?
Are they for the summer praying?—
    All is dead! dead! dead!

3.

Through the bushes, sadly swushing,
The blasts are frantic'ly rushing—
Their groans and cries never hushing:—
    All is dead! dead! dead!

4.

Dried leaves are hurriedly sweeping,
And o'er the ground crisp leaping;
A dull monotone keeping:—
    All is dead! dead! dead!

5.

The long gaunt trees are moaning,
And soft and dismally groaning—
Like bees sustainedly droning:—
    All is dead! dead! dead!

6.

The thaw on the ground is lying,
And mists o'er the hills are hieing—
Gray clouds through the air are flying.
       All is dead! dead! dead!

7.

Yet a breath of spring e'en now dwells in the air—
'Tis hope piercing through an age of despair.;
But this breath doth only more sadly declare:—
       All is dead! dead! dead!

8.

Yet soon will the spring come bounding along,
When nature again with beauty will throng;
Then no more shall be heard the dreary song:—
       All is dead! dead! dead!

LINES ON EDGAR ALLEN POE.

Poor Poe, though you now lie lowly,
Yet lives your Muse so melancholy.
When alive your heart was tender,
But drear as nature in December,
Yours was, in truth, a sorry lot,
One not to be so soon forgot.
The world to you was most unkind,
And to your merits stubborn blind.
By no one was you understood,
(Indeed who can know Genius' mood?)
So, 'stead of smiles you got a frown,
And sneers instead of laurel crown.
You was wretched, hungry, cold,
And suffered agonies untold.
But no one gave your wants attention,
Since your strait you would not mention.
Alas! though poor, yet you was proud,
And never spoke your hap aloud.
Since no one would your worth discern,

So no one's favor could you earn.
Then you grew gloomy and despairing;
Desperate—for nothing caring.
You took to drink to drown your woes,
And soon the grave o'er you did close.

Whoe'er has seen the Arctic clime,
Where nature's solitudes sublime—
Where earth is ghostly, grisly, weird—
Where men's hearts can ne'er be cheered?
The landscape there is dreary—grim;
And the skies are leaden—dim.
Yet there the winds, though keen, are pure,
And sweep o'er mountain and the moor
With wild and melancholy wailing—
To wake sadness never failing.
Snow covers all that vast bleak space,
And hides the verdure's ev'ry trace.
Yet 'neath those snows so crystalline

Slumber fires of devouring kind,
Whose flames arisen, having sway,
Burn and eat the hapless clay.

Poor Poe! thy Muse was just as chaste
As snows upon the Arctic waste.
The melancholy Northern sky,
Like thy music, makes us sigh.
Unconsciously thy notes complain
In a weird, unearthly strain.

Yet sleep thou soft, our own dear Poe;
For thou art safe from ev'ry woe.
Not one more pang nor one more care
Shall e'er again fall to thy share.
Though on earth thy task is ended—
Though thy clay with clay is blended—
Yet now thy long-neglected name
Is written in the Book of Fame.

ODE TO MELANCHOLY.

Thou seem'st to love me Goddess holy,
Calm and peaceful Melancholy!
Why dost thou so often woo me,
Giving to me pleasure gloomy?
I have parted from my mother,

From my father, sister, brother.
Altho' relatives surround me,
Their attentions serve to wound me.
I'm now of age, thank God, and free;
I care for none, none care for me.
My lot's my own, and I do choose
To dedicate it to the Muse.
Though all do sneer and tell me nay,
I do not care, I'll have my way.
My muse till now, was doomed to languish,
And my soul thus filled with anguish.
But freely now shall I express
The thoughts that I did long repress.

Alas! my boyhood days are fled,
And manhood's followed in their stead.
My youthful hopes were all vain dreams;—
My very nature altered seems.
When young, I thought the heavens blue,
Encompassed nought but what was true,
What people said would I believe,
And ne'er imagined, they'd deceive.
To me, life seemed a rosy dream,
A neverchanging happy scene.
All things on high, and here below,
Were parts, I thought, of one gay show.
That dream has vanished, sad to tell,
And what then was heaven now is hell.
I find that friendship's but a name—
A romance bright, but oh! how vain!
Sweet love, alas! is but a blind,
A lure to trick a foolish mind.
Men will lie and cheat for gain

Without the faintest blush of shame;
The fairest women oft lack virtue,
And try their utmost to pervert you.

Few poets seek the laurel crown—
They crave but riches or renown.
Patriotism's an illusion;
Politics a sad delusion.
Men love their country less than gain,
And placemen seek but power or fame;
He who is subtlest to deceive,
The greatest success will achieve.
He who can trick with mien most bold,
In men's regard gains firmest hold.
But why continue this recital?
It can bring one no requital.

No mortal will I love again;
For in my heart the Muse shall reign.
Beauty's charms no more shall sway me—
At least in this my heart'll obey me.
My dream of friendship, too, is o'er;
I once had friends—they're mine no more.
I've tried these friends, and found them wanting—
Their friendship's ghost my soul is haunting.
I'll walk alone o'er life's broad main,
Not sharing joy nor sharing pain;
I'll bear my burdens all alone,
And none shall ever hear me groan.
I own that once I did love fame,
And prized the glory of a name.
But what is fame? A gilded toy—
A plaything for a foolish boy.
Fame brings envy, malice, hate.
Are its rewards then adequate?
On nothing do I now set store—
Ambition dwells in me no more.
Men's pursuits seem little, vain;
And their existence—what's its aim?
Soon they'll die and be forgotten
Mayhap ere their corpse is rotten.

Come, I'll be joyous, heedless, gay,
And lightly thus pass life away.
Why hold the Muse in close subjection,
And numb my mind with deep reflection?
Why not strive to be in fashion,
And follow trifles with a passion?
Life then doth seem a pleasant play,
Continuing from day to day.
Yet, no! I scorn the fickle throng,
Which can't distinguish right from wrong.
It fawns and waits upon the great;
The poor, though, it doth cordial hate.
Misfortunes claims it don't allow—
To success only doth it bow.
How could I wear a smiling mood,
When tears would do me far more good?
Let those who will fawn and flatter,
I am made of blunter matter.
I do not heed public opinion,
And ne'er will bow to its dominion.
A straw for fashion's sick decrees!
I follow not the other geese.
Yet I do not despise mankind,
For.'mid the bad much good I find;
But I'll keep hidden in my shell
And watch the world around me well,
I'll cease wishing, hoping, sighing,
And only when I find I'm dying,
Will I call old Nick, and then,
I'll howl once more, and gasp Amen!

ESSAY.

ESSAY.

WHAT GENIUS IS.

Dr. Johnson says: "The true genius is a mind of large general powers accidentally determined to some particular direction."

This is an excellent general definition, yet not quite comprehensive enough.

Genius, according to my humble judgement, is neither more nor less than GREAT GOOD SENSE. Great good sense is an intellectual attribute—the result of a just equilibrium of all our faculties, spiritual and moral. It is a natural endowment and therefore opposed to everything artificial, circumstantial, or acquired. Furthermore, it is an altogether different quality from the mere sagacity of a lawyer or the shrewdness of a politician. It is in fact, the consentrated essence of many combined qualities.

Genius is not learning. Learning or knowledge is acquired, but genius (as beforesaid) is a natural endowment, or in other words, the gift of nature. Not all men of genius were educated. Improbable as it may seem, there have been men of genius who could neither read nor write. These men had a habit of reasoning more justly, and consequently of divining better than thousands of their fellow men, and therein lay the secret of their superiority. On the other hand a person may be ever so learned, but that does not render him a genius. Genius is a strangely wonderful thing, and is understood only by the happy possessor himself. The vast majority of mankind has not the faintest conception what it is. Learned men know no more about it than do uneducated people. It is an enigma to all but the initiated. Sir Bulwer Lytton says:

Genius, the Pythean of the Beautiful,
Leaves its large truths a riddle to the dull.
From eyes profane a vail the iris screens,
And fools on fools still asks what Hamlet means.

Wordsworth says:

Time, place, and action with pains may be wrought;
But genius must born, and never can be taught.

The multitude, not understanding what genius is, has no faith in its existence; and hence it is that men of genius are ever compelled to suffer the world's derision and abuse. Columbus, Galileo, Shakespeare, and in fact all men of greatest genius, were derided and abused from the mere fact of not being understood. There are men of mighty genius living to-day who have the same difficulties to contend against that Columbus and Galileo and Shakespeare have contended against before them. There are writers, musicians, sculptors, painters, actors, etc., living to-day, who are more or less endowed with the divine afflatus; yet they are so calumniated, vilified, and belittled by their fellow men that they lose all courage, and give up their undertakings in despair. The way they bear their trials, though, is a true test of their worth. If they have true genius, no obstacles, however great, will make them halt in their career, because the race-horse spirit of emulation urges them on against their will. They CANNOT halt, because a certain something, independent of their will, irresistibly impels them onward. But men of second-rate ability have not the true mettle, and when crossed in their career grow sulky and bad-tempered, and lose all ambition to win the goal. They believe success to be a game of chance, and then curse their ill-luck. They are short-sighted, though. Success is never won by chance. Genius wins success only by overcoming superhuman obstacles. Men of true genius bear their trials bravely, because they understand why humanity puts so many obstacles in their path. They perceive it is done from ignorance. I sincerely believe it to be the decree of a wise Providence that men of genius should bear the sticks, stones, and unhealthy eggs of non-appreciation, so that they may become purified and greater in the end. What atter days of cruel toil, nights of despondency, sickness, want, and all manner of suffering, when a glorious reward is to be gained at last?

To possess humanity's regard, affection, aye and even veneration forever—this is genius' reward. A sweeter reward no man can have.

The powers of a man of genius are general, and not confined to a particular sphere of action. He regards all matters, whether they relate to the sciences, arts, religions, business, or events in every-day life, with great good sense. He takes a common-sense view of everything.

There is a vast difference between him and a man of capacity or ability. A man of capacity or ability may become great by promulgating thoughts that he has acquired by study or observation, but a genius needs only to disclose his own original thought (acquired without effort) to win universal appreciation. A man of ability follows rules and precedents but a genius generally creates his own rules and laws. The former is an imitator, the latter is original. The laws and rules of any pursuit may be acquired by observation or study, and any man of ordinary capacity who possesses the qualities of speculation and abstraction may achieve good results by showing superior aptitude in that which he undertakes. Great praise is due to any man who by industry and study produces results to benefit the many. Yet such men though praiseworthy, are not to be compared to men of genius, because they are not capable of producing as great results. Since men of genius reason deeper, they can perceive results clearer, and, therefore, generally advance new ideas or make fresh discoveries. Men of ability, though, generally confine themselves to elaborating old truths.

A man of genius though not entirely dependent upon art for success is materially benefitted by it. Art implies a disposition of mind to use artificial means to attain an end. Genius discovers the thought and art dresses it in becoming raiment. To achieve the highest results both are very much dependent upon each other.

Men of genius never know that the divine afflatus lives within them, till it is revealed to turn by others or by a chance circumstance. An author, for instance, delineates the character of a man of genius in his book which bears a close resemblance to the reader's own. The reader finds that the person portrayed in the book has the same habits of thought and conduct that he has, and that he is in fact a perfect counterpart of himself; he sees his own soul reflected as in a mirror. Thus he learns to know himself. The chrysalis of his genius remained undeveloped in its shell till an accidental ray of light gave it warmth and being. An undefined feeling told him that he was born to soar, yet he knew not how. At last there came the ray of light which awoke him to life and action, and then his genius took wing and soared to heaven freely, boldly and confidently.

Men of genius were born to lead their fellow men. They are the prophets of humanity, and are second only to that mysterious worker, that men call God.

TRAVELS.

TRAVELS.

MY TRAVELS IN GERMANY.

It was in the smiling month of May, of the year 1868, when my father, mother, six brothers and sisters, and our nurse embarked on the North German Lloyd steamship " Deutschland," for Bremen. I was but a small boy then, 13 years of age, and the thought of making a trip to Europe made me feel mighty as an Emperor. How I swaggered and bragged, and put on heaps of airs to show my importance to the other small boys, I will not now stop to relate. Suffice it to say I felt good all over.

We embarked on the " Deutschland," as beforesaid. I strode up and down the deck of the stately vessel and studied her anatomy intently. After a thorough investigation I concluded that I would love to live on her forever. I remarked as much to my father, who only smiled at my simplicity. I asked a sailor, who was coiling a rope on the steerage deck, why there was so many cords tied to the mast aloft. Was it to keep the masts from falling overboard? The sailor grinned at me, and said, " Of course!"

Soon the vessel slowly glided out from her pier. At first I thought it was the pier that was deserting us, but, as the vessel swung out into the river, I found that the pier had not budged. I stood on deck holding my hat in one hand and a handkerchief in the other waving them both to our friends on the pier and shouting " good-bye! good-bye! hooray! hooray!" At last our friends' faces were no longer to be distinguished in the crowd, and I turned to gaze upon the scenery of New York Bay. The day was fair—a fairer one never dawned—and everything was correspondingly lovely The environs of New York never seemed more beautiful, though they are always beauti-

ful and interesting. We passed Castle Garden, Gov-
ernor's Island, Brooklyn, Bay Ridge, Fort Hamilton,
and Fort Richmond, and then our noble vessel, grace-
fully gliding through the narrows, passed Coney
Island and Staten Island. Ere long Sandy Hook, the
last point of land was passed, and then the broad and
heaving ocean lay before us. What a glorious specta-
cle it was! Grand! noble! magnificent! The vessel
began to heave a little now, and I began to feel "kind
of funny," so I told my father. Ere long I began to
feel funnier still, for things did not seem half as lovely
as before. I experienced sea sickness now for the
first time. I did not like it all. I howled with fear,
and wished I had never seen the plaguey mean ship.
It was the ship's fault that I was sick, I thought,
because she could have been made to stop rolling.
I wasn't the only one in our family, though, who was
sea-sick, and that thought was a great comfort to me.
Soon as the last point of land faded from view my
mother grew frightened at the prospect of endless sky
and water, and hastened to her cabin with all speed.
She cast herself upon the bed, and, in spite of all
arguments and entreaties, would not stir from it till
she was assured, after ten days, that the coast of
England was in sight. When she saw the land fade
away far in the distance, and naught about us but
sky and water, the thought came to my mother that
if anything happened to the ship we would be miles
and miles away from help. The thought was terrible,
and now to heighten her misery came sea-sickness
beside. My mother was a much-abused lady then
there was no doubt of it. Had the ocean withheld its
tortures she might have overcome other ills, but old
Neptune cares for nobody, not even for my mother.
Our nurse, when she first stepped on board, felt de-
lighted as myself with the ship, but, alas! her rapture,
like mine, soon gave way to misery. When the vessel
began heaving, she pressed her hand against her stom-
ach and said, "Oh! oh!" in heart melting tones. Ere long
she wished herself dead, or that she had never seen
us because then she would never have been on this
horrid old tub of a boat. My father felt not the least

twinge of sea-sickness, nor did any of my younger
brothers and sisters. That I, the oldest of them all,
should be sick, did not seem right to me. After a few
days had passed, I felt all right again. Most of the
time was passed on deck, where sea quoits, novel
reading, and sight-seeing were indulged in. After
ten days had passed a dim haze was seen by us upon
the extreme verge of the horizon, and this the captain
assured us was land. Once more I took my hat in hand
and cried hooray till I grew hoarse. With that
glimpse of land my gay spirits returned to me. The
outlines of a rock-bound coast soon burst upon my
admiring vision. It was the coast of England. Any
land would have been welcome to me then, but a
FOREIGN land was doubly welcome. "Hip, hip,
hooray!" cried I enthusiastically, and flung my hat to
the breeze, which nearly carried it overboard.

In due course of time we anchored off Cowes, Isle of
Wight. A breeze from shore was wafted to us laden
with the smell of grass and flowers. It was salubri-
ous. It quickened my pulses and braced my nerves,
and I strode up and down the deck feeling strong as a
lion. We anchored off Cowes for the night. The
night came on quickly, and the stars came forth one
by one. There was no moon. The reed-covered shore
was but a biscuit-toss away, and it loomed up black in
the gloaming. Narrow black-painted boats, carrying
a green light at the bow and a yellow one at the stern,
gracefull, glided past our vessel. Not far from us the
hulls of schooners and lighters could dimly be dis-
cerned. On shore, lights were seen in every direction.
Taken as a whole, the scene was a romantic one. It
conjured up old Venice to my imagination, and I won-
dered whether that famous city of the sea could pre-
sent a scene half so entrancing as this. I did not
retire to bed that night, but remained on deck to sur-
feit myself with the sights. All was so novel and in-
teresting to me that I could not sleep. Old Sol arose
next morning smiling and blushing, and presented new
pictures. Tall, bright-green blades of sea-grass, that
lined the shore, were wet with huge dewdrops, and as
the sunrays touched them they reflected all the colors

of the rainbow. And upon the good Queen's marine palace at Cowes, the Osborne House, Old Sol boldly cast his rays. First he burnished one window, then he took the same liberty with another, and another, and another, till every one of the many windows became flashing, dazzling mirrors of light. It was, in truth, a gorgeous spectacle.

As the morning wore on we hove up our anchor again, and steamed for Bremerhaven, our destination. Having arrived there, a tug came alongside to tow the "Deutschland" to her pier. The awkward Germans on board the tug seemed sorely distressed how to heave a rope on board our vessel. They ran back and forth aimlessly, like cockroaches in distress. Finally, they gathered in assembly upon the bow of their boat, to determine definitely upon a proper course of action. They decided to tie a small line to a large line, and then to toss the small line on board our ship. Their tact, shrewdness, and skill rendered them successful in the end, and we applauded them in a becoming manner. They did not acknowledge our civility, however.

Bremerhaven now claimed our attention. The town —a seaport—is old, battered, and time-stained. The houses are rickety and crickety and black, dirty and seedy-looking. Their roofs are huge and slanting as a young mountain. And then they cling to each other with deepest affection. Should one of these dirty-looking time pets withdraw his loving support from his neighbor, what a fall there then would be. What boards, and beams, and gables and spires, and nooks and crannies, and dirt and grime would at last take a tumble! What a sad contemplation that would be for the townspeople. If that event was to happen, then new houses would have to be built, and new houses mean change and cleanliness, evils, alas! to which the conservative people of Bremerhaven are not accustomed.

As we set foot on shore we found a railroad train waiting to convey us to Bremen. I was much amused to see the little twopenny engine and the old-fashioned stage-coach cars that composed the train. The cars soon moved away from the depot and clatter, clatter, clattered toward Bremen. In due time we arrived at that city. "Jiminy Gripes! what a strange place it is!" thought I. We engaged a fiacre (or a couple of them I think) and were hurried to the Hotel de l'Europe, where the family soon was made comfortable.

Then my father, brother, and myself started out for a stroll. The streets were narrow and quaint-looking. There were numerous shops over which signs, bearing terrible hard names to pronounce, were creaking and groaning in the wind. Strange looking people wearing strange garments and using strange language were met with everywhere. I did not hear a single word of English spoken. Everyone—from the dirty faced street arab to the staid and sober merchant—spoke German. I was more than surprised—I was astonished. "Here is something to tell the New York boys when I see them," thought I. Ere long I discovered something that nearly left me breathless with interest and delight. It was a windmill, something that I had read much about but never seen. And here it was with its four black stilt-like legs, its black, fat little body and its four huge arms continually sawing the air. I importuned my father to lead us into it. In those days my father granted my lightest wish, so into the windmill we went. The miller, though surprised that any one should feel interested in so common a thing as a mill, received us courteously. He led us about the structure and took much pains to explain everything connected therewith to us. The mill room was low and rather confined, yet to me it seemed so cosy and homelife that I would have loved to live in it forever. We mounted a stairway and found ourselves close to the roof. Through an aperture the huge fans or arms could be seen tossing upward outside the building. There was an incessant creak, creak of the fans and a hum, hum, hum below stairs. After having satisfied our curiosity we thanked the miller for his attention and departed.

We next wended our way to a Rathskeller! A Rathskeller is a vault or series of vaults where beer

and a variety of good things can be had for the mere
payment thereof. These vaults are much like the
underground passages of a convent or dungeon. They
are paved with flagstones, and contain massive pillars.
Successive rows of arches reach into the dim distance.
Upon these arches are graven or inscribed legends
from mythology or witty verses from the German lit-
erature. We ordered "drei portion" bread, butter,
cheese, and beer. The beer which was served in stone
jugs was sparkling and delicious as the morning dew.
I emptied my jug without winking and smacked my
lips with satisfaction. My father said I would be-
come a first-class Dutchman in time. I burst into
loud and prolonged laughter. My father thought that
I was laughing at his remark, but I was not. The
fumes of the beer had mounted to my brain and made
me feel queer. All eyes were turned upon me, but I
gazed intently at the inscriptions upon the arches, and
thus the good-natured assemblage present deemed
them the cause of my merriment. I laughed louder
and louder, and the people present were no doubt grat-
ified to think that I could apprec.ate ancient jokes.
Not till long afterward did the effects of the beer
wear off. I was glad when we emerged from the
vault to the bright daylight again.

Our stroll was continued. We did not walk far
when we came upon the market-place of the town.
Here was another surprise for me. Instead of being
under cover, the market was held in the open street, a
large square being devoted to that purpose. Baskets
containing wares of all kinds were placed on the side-
walks, in the roadway, and in all manner of convenient
and inconvenient places. Each basket was presided
over by an enterprising dame. Fruits, vegetables, but-
ter, cheese, milk, eggs, bologna sausages, live fishes in
tubs of water, smoked meats, live geese, chickens, ducks,
etc., were here in profusion. The market women were
bargaining noisily, and kept up a ceaseless chatter and
squabbling, in which the geese and other fowl joined.
It was, in truth, an animated scene. I purchased two
grotes worth of cherries from one of the market la-
dies, and, beside the cherries, received a most bewitch-

ing smile from her. The smile alone was worth two
grotes. The lady did not make any extra charge for
it, however. There was a lady here who presided over
a basket containing a curious kind of cheese. I was
not long in scraping an acquaintance with her. The
lady's name was Maria something, and the cheese's
name was handkase. I tasted the cheese and found it
heavenly. "Dutchmen know what is good, anyway!"
said I to myself. Our family remained an entire week
at Bremen, and thus I had many an opportunity to
court the handkase lady's society. She always received
me with a pleasant word of welcome. I thought con-
siderable of her—looked upon her, in fact, as an old
friend. She told me she made these handkase herself,
and then my regard for her was boundless. Bremen
held not her equal. Upon the last day of our stay at
Bremen, I came to her and said: "Madam, our family
leaves for Frankfort-on-the-Main to-day, where my
brother and myself are to be put at school. I may
never see you again, so please give me your best hand-
kase!" She gave me the cheese, then hurriedly car-
ried the corner of a dirty apron to her eye and drew
several prolonged snuffles through her nose. She was
crying, I thought. I tried to comfort her. "PLEASE
don't cry, madam. I'll come to Bremen some day or
other and see you again; see if I don't!" The effect of
this little speech was electric upon her. She took the
apron from her eye and not a trace of emotion was vis-
ible upon her countenance. She gave me the last
handkase, placed her huge paw in mine and said
"adieu!"

> Old dame, when I meet thee,
> After many years,
> How shall I greet thee?

I shall greet thee with the same affection as of
yore. Count on me!

The ride from Bremen to Frankfort-on-Main, in the
railroad cars, was an interesting one. I will stop to
relate an incident of it. Our family took possession of
a second-class coupe, in which there was a solitary
passenger, who looked upon our intrusion as an inva-
sion of his rights. This solitary passenger was a stout

middle aged merchant bound for Frankfort. We
children were very noisy, so he squeezed himself into
a corner far from us as possible Notwithstanding
our noise, and notwithstanding the rackety-clackety
noise of the train, he soon fell asleep and snored
loudly. Above his head was a rack which contained
our portable language. Among our effects was a bas-
ket of peaches which the younger children clamored
for. I mounted upon an arm of the seat and took the
basket from the rack. Unfortunately I slipped and
brought the basket of peaches down with stunning
force upon the stout gentleman's uncovered head.
He shot up like a rocket and exclaimed: "Kreuz, Ge-
witter, Donner, Wetter was ist das?,' He glared at
me and rubbed his head vigorously. My parents apol-
ogized for my awkwardness, and used their best efforts
to mollify him. He accepted the apology and was
easily appeased, but his actions when struck had been
so comical that every now and again I burst into un-
controllable fits of laughter. I was reprimanded, yet
I could not control my merriment. As we neared
Frankfort, however, my merriment subsided. My
brother and I were to be put to school here for three
years. Our parents were to leave us at Frankfort,
and after seeing sights on the continent were to re-
turn to New York, our home, The idea did not please
me at all. I asked my father what would become of
us if we were left alone among these savage foreign-
ers. My father replied: "I do not know, I am sure!"
This answer was far from consoling, and my mind
grew troubled. A dark cloud of apprehension
settled over me, and all my gay spirits fled. Not even
the many interesting sights we saw as we entered
Frankfort, could rouse me. After our family had
been made cozy at an hotel in Frankfort, my father,
mother, brother and myself rode to the school in a
fiacre. The school-house which was situated on the
Bruckhofstrasse, was a plain three-story granite build-
ing. In my then frame of mood it seemed to me
grim and ominous looking. We ascended a long flight
of stone steps, and were ushered by a servant into a
cozy reception-room. Mr. and Mrs. Blank, the propri-

etors of the boarding-school (at Frankfort called a
pension) were there to meet us. Mr. Blank (his real
name I omit) was rather a short, thickset gentleman,
having a close-clipped, ruddy beard, a frank and pleas-
ing countenance, and wore gold-rimmed spectacles.
At that time (the year 1868) he was about 40 years
of age. Mrs. Blank was also below the medium
size, having brown hair that was smoothed back
from her forehead, penetrating gray eyes, and heavy
jaw; around her waist was tied a bunch of keys and a
pair of scissors which gave her a housewifely appear-
ance. Mr. Blank and his wife received us kindly.
Arrangements for our board, tuition, &c., were soon
completed. After a prolonged chat our parents rose
to depart. We received a few necessary hints, such as
to behave well, to obey Mr. and Mrs. Blank in every-
thing to be diligent in our studies, to write home re-
gularly, &c., &c., and then our parents kissed us adieu
and with the rest of the family that evening set off
for Paris. The dread event had come to pass then;
we were left to the tender mercies of savage foreigners.
A storm was gathering in my breast. After our par-
ents had departed Mr. Blank in person conducted us to
the room my brother and I were to occupy. The room
was furnished with two beds, two chairs, one wash-
ing basin, and a bureau. There were forty pensioners
in the school beside my brother and I. Mr. Blank left
us. I felt homesick, sad and dispirited. I threw my-
self upon the bed and then the storm which had long
been pent up, burst in all its fury. I yelled as though
I was being murdered. My brother felt calm and un-
ruffled as though he had been at school in Frankfort
all his life. He told me to stop yelling. I yelled
louder than before. Mr. Blank rushed up in alarm.
"What ails you, my lad?" asked he. "I don't want to
stay in this nasty old school, I want to go to Paris
with my parents," sobbed I. "Console yourself, my
lad," said Mr. Blank, "you will go to Paris some fine
day with all the boys here to see the sights. This did
not comfort me much and I bawled loud as ever. Soon
I heard eager voices whispering to each other outside
the door. A delegation of students were there inter-

ested to know whether I was being thrashed so soon.
One student remarked: "What a yell that was: I
wonder do *all* the New York Indians yell like that?"
My brother heard the remark and it riled him. He
stepped out into the corridor and demanded to know
who passed that remark. The students did not un-
derstand my brother who spoke in English (he could
not speak a word of German) therefore none answered
him. My brother misinterpreted their silence and
scowled at them to show his contempt for their sup-
posed cowardice. One of the students asked my
brother in broken English; "for why you make so?"
imitating his scowl. My brother who thought the
student was deriding him planted a blow on his ear by
way of answer. There was a lively scene then. All
the students gesticulated excitedly and shouted to
their comrade: "Druf Albert! Druf!" (At him Al-
bert! At him!) Albert did not know whether *all*
American chaps carried pistols and bowie knives so he
hesitated. My brother remarked to him in a confident
manner: "I can thrash a dozen Dutchmen like you!"
Fortunately Albert did not understand the remark
or he might have been more frightened than he was.
The other students urged him on to the slaughter.
Albert gritted his teeth and sailed into the fray. He
bit, scratched, kicked and poked my brother in the ribs
with his thumbs. My brother struck right out from
the shoulder. At last Albert received a blow in the
eye that made him see little green blazes and it sick-
ened him. He slunk away utterly discomfited. The
other students set up a howl of commiseration and
intended to fall upon my brother in a body, but he
wisely ran into our room, and told Mr. Blank, who
stepped into the corridor and dispersed the angry
crowd.

There were young men from many countries in the
pension. There were about a dozen Americans,
English, French, Italian, and German lads; also one
Wallachian. Many took private lessons at home in
the pension, while others attended preparatory schools
and universities. I took private lessons at home, but
my brother attended a preparatory school sweetly

called the Philantropina. There were several quaint characters among the students, one of whom I will stop to describe. The lad I have reference to came from Manchester, England, and his front name was Ted. We nicknamed him "Spleenisher Englander" (spleenetic Englishman) because he was so soft. He would believe anything that was told him. Many were the tricks that were played upon him. One nights several students chalked their faces, wrapped long sheets around their bodies, rubbed sulphur upon their foreheads, and, with long-bladed knives gleaming in their hands, stalked into Ted's room. The coverlet was roughly pulled off him, and he was given a sounding thwack with a stick upon a very delicate spot. He jumped up in a hurry, but when he saw the ghostly figures standing by his bedside erect and silent, he hastily pulled the clothes over himself and gave a blood curdling shriek. The ghosts tried to pull the coverlet from him again, but Ted clung to it desperately. A pitcher of water was thrown over him, whereupon he set up a series of shrieks that could have been heard blocks away. The ghosts fled precipitately then, stumbling over each other in their eagerness to get away before Mr. Blank caught them. This was one of the tricks played upon him. One day Ted told a comrade that he had broken his lorgrette (like most Englishmen he sported an eyeglass) and that he accidentally swallowed a large piece of glass. Immediately his comrade, who was a wag, assumed a serious air, and told Ted that swallowing a piece of glass was a highly dangerous thing to do. "Suppose that glass should work itself to your heart, Ted, why you will be dead in less than an hour." Ted grew frightened. "Tell me what shall I do, Siegfried," said he to the wag distressedly. Siegfried, after thinking a moment or two, said: "If you faithfully promise to do as I say I'll rid you of that glass." Ted faithfully promised to do what he was bidden. "Get a large bottle of cod liver oil over at the druggist's, and no matter whether your liver comes up or not drink it all, else you will be a dead lad in less than no time. Ted bought the oil and brought it to Siegfried. Ted tested it and shuddered. " Ugh! I cawn't go that," said he. " You must," persisted Siegfried. Ted held his nostrils shut so as not to smell the vile stuff, and drank the entire contents of the bottle. A delegation of students called upon him next morning in his room, where he lay sick in bed, and asked him how he felt. " Very bad," said the poor fellow. "But is the glass up ?" anxiously inquired his fellow students with long drawn faces. "I cawn't say, you know, I did not stop to see!" It took him several days to get over the effects of that bottle.

There were some other droll characters in the school beside Ted, but I will not stop to describe them. My brother and I found the students to be a jolly set when we came to understand their ways and habits.

Each Sunday in the year, the younger students took a walk with Mr. Blank to some place of interest near Frankfort. Whenever it rained on a Sunday, we adjourned to some cafe in the suburbs of the town, where we drank beer, ate cakes, and listened to the sweet strains of a band of music. In fine weather we walked to the woods near Frankfort, gathering nuts, playing games, and amusing ourselves generally. Once each year Mr. Blank and as many students as chose, made tours of some length. Some of the tours lasted a day or two, others an entire week. Among the places visited were Baden Baden, Wiesbaden, Homburg, Cologne, the Rhine, Switzerland, etc. I will describe one of these tours.

The first tour that my brother and I made in company with the students, was to Wiesbaden and Homburg.

We all arose long before daylight on the day of the tour, and felt happy as clam at high tide. We swallowed our coffee and brodchen (rolls) in hot haste, slung our knapsacks—botamsirbuchsen, we called them—upon our backs, and were soon ready to depart. The command to depart ere long was given, and we hurried through the dark, deserted streets of Frankfort to the Bahnhof (railroad station), where we were to take the cars for Wiesbaden. We entered the station and made a rush for the cars. There was much

struggling among us for reserved seats in the cars—
the seats nearest the windows. As the cars moved
away from the station our "hochs" (hurrahs) were
deafening to hear. We had to vent our enthusiasm
some way. After about an hour's ride we reached
Wiesbaden. Though the day had not yet dawned, we
overran the town like a horde of wild Arabs, shout-
ing, whooping, and yelling. Wiesbaden, though a
small, is a picturesque town, nestling at the base of
verdure-clad mountains. The scenery around it is
charming. The town was dark and silent, its inhabi-
tants being wrapped in slumber. When we had gained
the town limits and just as we were about to ascend
the mountain, we came upon a number of saddle-don-
keys reclining on the sward. Their drivers lay
stretched out at full length, wrapped up in blankets,
not far away from them. We roused the drivers
and tried to make some arrangement with them about
hiring all their donkeys for a ride up the mountain.

After much gesticulating, shouting, and bargaining,
we came to satisfactory terms. The donkeys were
called up from the places where they were reclining.
They seemed unwilling to be disturbed from their rest
so early. There were not enough donkeys for all of us
so it was agreed among us to take turns. We h ad
some difficulty in mounting the brutes. They w ere
ugly and refractory, and needed to be coaxed. We
coaxed them with canes, switches, and umbrellas, but
they seemed insensible to such cajoling. Their dri-
vers whacked them unmercifully and shouted " hi ! hi !
hi !" but they heeded the drivers as little as they did
us. I had mounted a big mule and his nasty nature
awoke my ire. I broke my cane upon his back but he
only playfully whisked his tail. I yelled at him, pet-
ted him, coaxed him, but he was oblivious to every-
thing. I then stuck a pin into him and he rose upon
his hind legs and gave vent to a series of brays that
struck terror into my heart. I slid off his back in a
hurry and could not be induced to mount him again.
Ted was one of the would-be riders. He bestrode a
diminutive donkey—scarcely big as himself—but the
animal was stubborn as a mule. Ted twisted his tail,

pinched his ear, and poked him in the ribs with his
umbrella, but produced no other effect than to make
him hee-haw. The unmounted students watched his
proceedings with much interest. Without speaking a
word they all innocently gathered around his donkey.
Suddenly a shower of blows fell upon the brute and
made it rear. A lit cigarette was then placed under
its tail. It gave a loud snort and a jump and then tore
up the mountain side in a frantic manner. Ted clung
to it in terror, but dropped his eye-glass. "Mein zwic-
ker! mein zwicker!" (My eye-glass! my eye-glass!)
he shouted frantically. The donkey did not care a
cent for him or his eye-glass, but continued in its mad
career.

The rest of the caravan now had started and fol-
lowed Ted's donkey up the mountain leisurely. The
day had not fully dawned, and a stiff breeze was blow-
ing. Away far up we could see huge clouds gallivant-
ing around the mountain top. Soon we reached the
top where we waited for the walkers of our party to
arrive. Ted had reached the summit long before us.
"Well, Ted, is the donkey alive yet?" was asked.
"Blarst the bloody donkey," said he, "I thought sure
he'd break my neck coming up!" After a little our
entire party had assembled. A chapel, patterned after
the Greek style, was built on the mountain top. A
lovelier and at the same time a wilder spot could not
have been selected for it. There was no other build-
ing within miles of it. We rang up the chapel ward-
en, who admitted us into the building. The chapel
was built of finest marble and had many deep-set,
high, variegated glass windows. The golden sunbeams
illumined the stained glass and cast many hues—
orange, green, purple, yellow, white, and red—upon a
marble figure representing her grace the Grand Duch-
ess Van der Blinkenhoven Van der Blankensteim (I
forgot her last name), of Kurhessen. Her grace's ef-
figy was reclining at full length on a raised marble
bier. As a work of art, it possessed much merit.
Some of the students were excellent art critics—in
their own minds—and critically examined the Duchess.
One critic remarked, "Sie ist hubsch zum kissen" (she

is lovely enough to kiss). Another said: "Her features are faultless, with the exception of that wart on her chin," which proved to be a fly. Ted said she was "pawfectly grand." After all had sufficiently ogled the duchess and inspected the chapel to their hearts' content, we departed. Those who had not ridden the donkeys before, now had their turn. Going down was far more exciting than coming up. The donkeys scampered down the mountain side at a lively rate, and their riders bounced up and down upon their backs like india rubber balls. One tall and lanky German lad was flung headlong over his donkey's head and was gathered up more dead than alive. When picked up, he asked in a dazed manner, "Wo bin ich?" (where am I?), to which a would-be wag replied: "Auf dein hinterviertel" (upon your hindquarters), whereupon the lanky lad showed his teeth and looked fight. Even when town was reached the donkeys would not stop, but galloped through the streets at the top of their speed. A crowd of street boys ran after them, shouting, whooping and yelling. This maddened the donkeys. They charged through every street in the town, one following the other, and would not halt till compelled to from sheer exhaustion. None of the students were ever after anxious to go donkey riding.

After we had all assembled again it was unanimously decided that breakfast ought to be the next event on the programme. Accordingly we all repaired to the nearest inn where an ample repast was soon spread before us. What with appetites sharpened by the bracing mountain air, and what with the lively exercise we had taken we felt hungry enough to have devoured all the provisions in Wiesbaden. Our good natured host and his assistants had all they could do to attend to our wants.

Breakfast being over we took a short rest and then strolled through the town leisurely to see what we could see. Wiesbaden is one of the watering places of Germany and strangers flock here from far and near to drink the health-giving waters and for recuperation generally. It was then the height of the season. It was now about 10 o'clock a. m., and the streets were full of people. People from all nations were here to be met with. There were Englishmen, Frenchmen, Austrians, Spaniards, Americans. Italians, Turks, &c., &c. It was an aristocratic and well-dressed crowd, too, with little or none of the riff-raff element.

We wended our way to the Kur Gardens. Such a grand sight we students never saw before. The gardens are scarcely less lovely than the famous Versailles Gardens. Both nature and art have combined to render them beautiful. Lordly elms, larches, beeches, chestnut and cedar trees studded the gardens and afforded a grateful shade. Then there were well-graveled walks that led to every direction. Parterres of flowers, laid out with much skill and taste, charmed the eye, and the many-colored sweet-smelling flowers almost intoxicated the senses with their perfume. Fountains that threw up jets of water more than 100 feet high were plentiful. Under a cluster of trees a handsome pavilion was built; in it a band of music was in the habit of playing twice each day, at 10 A. M. and 4 P. M. In every direction well-dressed ladies, gentlemen, and children were promenading. Princes, Dukes, Counts, Barons, Generals, Colonels, Ministers, Statesmen, and other high-toned personages, were plentiful as bedbugs in a boarding-house. Fat dowagers were taking an airing in company with their pet poodles. English mammas, attired in elegant morning costumes, and surrounded by flaxen-haired, chubby-faced, prattling children, were leisurely walking about. Then there were Austrian matrons, with complexions fresh and blooming as a red rose. French ladies you could see, attired in that simple yet elegant manner that they so well know how to excel in. They were elegant, refined, and courtly in their manners. and were gayly chatting and laughing. What delicious nothings issued from those ruby lips, and what *espeglerie*, grace, wit, and sentiment they possessed! Ye lovely dames of France, I kiss the tips of your fingers with admiration! Dusky, dark-eyed ladies from Spain and Italy could be seen and heard conversing in those rich, soft, and flowing accents so very like music. They called forth visions of their own sunny lands, where all is poetry, music, sunlight, sentiment, and luxurious delight. There were bravely accoutred officers from all nations here, too, upon whose breasts gleamed medals and decorations innumerable, and who fraternized in the most familiar manner.

In the grounds were cafes, restaurants, and refreshment pavillions, which were thronged with people. People were seated at the tables eating ices, drinking light wines, and feasting generally. The jingle of glasses, the clatter of plates, the rattle of knives and forks, the drinking and gormandising, the laughter and conversation reminded one forcibly of the boulevards of Paris. To carry out the illusion, active French waiters, arrayed in black frock coats, white ties, and spotless linen, moved about among the throng with well laden trays, and now and then gave vent to a sacre God damn between their teeth when some one jostled them too rudely. Soon we entered the gaming halls, which were then at the height of their iniquitous glory. The halls—there were several of them—were frescoed, bepainted, and bedizened. Costly, elaborate wrought chandeliers depended from the ceilings, supporting amber hued globes, within which were low burning lights that diffused a golden glow throughout the apartment. The furniture was rich and sumptuous, so rich and sumptuous that I was afraid to sit down on one of the sofas for fear of committing sacrilege. Fine paintings relieved the monotony of bare walls, and statuary occupied the niches. The balmy morning air stole in through the open windows and mingled with the soft perfumes pervading the apartments. The floors were of high polished illuminated woods, and in their center stood the gaming tables. Distinguished looking ladies and gentlemen were already, so early in the morning, engaged in the various games of chance. Many a titled profligate was seated at these tables a perfect slave to the passion of gambling. Nor were profligates of the gentler sex lacking to complete the high-toned depravity of the scene. Some of the latter were as inveterate gamblers as the former. Many spectators stood around the tables engaged in watching the proceedings. Conversation was not allowed, and the silence was only broken by the click click of the roulette wheel, the croupier's calls of the game, and the clink clink clink of gold and silver. In one hall roulette was played, in another rouge et noir, in still another vingt et un, etc. The faces of the players betrayed not a single emotion. Whether they lost or won their faces wore its calm impertubable expression. Their self-control was wonderful. A beautiful lady player particularly engaged my attention. I watched her as she gradually lost thousands of thalers. First her huge piles of gold and silver were swept in, then bank note upon bank note till not a sou remained. The lady gracefully arose then, without a trace of emotion being visible in her lovely countenance, and walked away, whereupon her chair was immediately occupied by another noble patron of the art. I cannot describe my feelings while witnessing this scene. The lady's beauty had dazzled me, her wealth had awed me, and her command over herself won my admiration, and when she staked her last bank note I held my breath in suspense. When it was swept away I groaned and would have fallen. A disgust for gamblers of whatever sex then possessed me. Those play halls have long since been abolished by a decree of Kaiser Wilhelm. A sensible old Kaiser that.

The next place we traveled to was Homburg. At Homburg there was a castle of ye ancient days, a something which I had long been pining for to see. I had read Anna Radcliffe's "Mysteries of Udolpho," and other high-wrought, glowing romances, till my fancy was worked up to a high pitch of interest. When I stood within the time-honored walls of that Homburg castle, my enthusiasm knew no bounds. I felt awe-stricken, and my flesh began to creep. Each individual hair stood on end and to express myself in one word I felt "alloverish!" I felt capable then and there of writing a romance than which even Miss Anna Radcliffe never wrote a more thrilling one.

We first inspected the long and venerable castle hall. It was a vast apartment full of old armor, weapons, and the like. The casements, which were lofty, reaching to the ceiling almost, and were open to admit fresh air. Without could be seen lordly elms, and chestnut trees, that were softly soughing and swirring in the gentle summer breeze. They roused my fancy and I thought they were whispering to each other about the deeds of daring performed by the castle owners in ages gone by. They conjured up visions of courtly knights and lovely dames, and troubadours, and roystering soldiers. We passed through other halls, apartments, rooms, and, also, dungeons. I was charmed and delighted with everything. It was many a long day before the effects of the visit to the castle was effaced from my brain.

I have omitted many things in this sketch. I have described little of our school-life, little of Frankfort, itself, and little of anything in fact. I may make amends in the future, perhaps. My sketch, such as it is, is done.

www.ingramcontent.com/pod-product-compliance
Lightning Source LLC
Chambersburg PA
CBHW031750090426
42739CB00008B/955